For Your Enjoycement

THE REMOVAL OF PADDY DIGNAM

Loosely Based on Episode *Six* of *Ulysses*

THE REMOVAL

For Your Enjoycement

OF PADDY DIGNAM

Loosely Based on Episode Six of *Ulysses*

Written and illustrated by SEÁN LENNON

with a *Foreword* by DAVID NORRIS, Senator and Joycean Scholar

First published 2004 by
FINGAL COUNTY LIBRARIES
Dublin • Ireland
www.fingalcoco.ie

*This book is dedicated to the memory of
Kathleen and Molly Lennon.*

Acknowledgements

The author would like to thank: Paul Harris, the Fingal County Librarian, for his encouragement and interest in this book, from inception to completion; Senator David Norris, the best and most eloquent of Joyce's champions, for his Foreword; David Butler of the James Joyce Centre whose assistance I have enjoyed; Alan Moore and Anvil Press Poetry for permission to quote from *Fluntern*; Susan Waine for producing another dream design in her expert and informed way; Yvonne O'Reilly and the staff of Fingal Libraries who were always welcoming, supportive and full of valuable suggestions. I have in fact had a good deal of help and am particularly indebted to the following: Miriam Gordon, Gerard Dockery, Peter Somers, John Hackett, Yvonne O'Brien, Michael Carrick, James Rickard, Stephen Redmond S.J., and Brian Sayers. I am so grateful to Bill and Bob for their continuing assistance. Without the light of drawing this world would be a dull old place. Special thanks to Maureen Lennon, who taught me how to draw, for this latest set of illuminations (look Mam, 2 books in 7 months!). She's helping me 'up there', I know. *The Removal of Paddy Dignam* has cast me in the role of unchosen collaborator with one of the finest novelists of the last century, who I might also wish to thank! However, my deepest thanks go to my family, Anne, Aisling, and Cormac Lennon.

Set in 14 on 17 point Nicolas Cochin
Designed by SUSAN WAINE Printed in Ireland by JOHNSWOOD PRESS LIMITED DUBLIN

It is with great pleasure that I introduce Seán Lennon's latest book of drawings, inspired on this occasion by chapter 6 of *Ulysses*. Dublin has seen many changes since Leopold Bloom first walked its streets, and the time is right to revisit some of the landmark buildings included in Joyce's text. Seán Lennon is the ideal person to take us on such a journey. Fingal Libraries is commited to engaging with the community through cultural activity and we are delighted to publish *The Removal of Paddy Dignam* as our contribution to the Bloomsday centenary celebrations.

PAUL HARRIS
Fingal County Librarian

Foreword

Joyce's view of Dublin might be described as bifocal since he had what could be called a divided opinion about his native city, both loving and hating it simultaneously. He skipped the hell out of it when he was in his early twenties and although he visited it once or twice after that from his continental exile, (most notably in 1909 when he opened Dublin's first cinema 'The Volta') he never came back at all after the age of 30. However, when he was asked when, if ever, he would return to Dublin, he replied oracularly "Have I ever left it?" and he would regularly engage visitors from Dublin in a kind of mastermind quiz about the street life of Dublin. In this little game the participants were required to name all the shops on Dublin's principal streets up one side and down the other. Joyce himself of course invariably won.

He would have a lot of catching up to do these days because a good deal has changed. One classic example would be the old Ballast Office on the southern side of O'Connell Bridge. This was demolished quite a number of years ago and a modern office building put up with a replica façade. However the new owners resited the old clock from the Westmoreland Street side of the building to the quay side thus creating consternation among oriental Joycean scholars who puzzled their heads to work out

by DAVID NORRIS Senator and Joycean Scholar

how Stephen standing in Westmoreland Street could actually see the clock at all in its new reincarnation. I suppose that would qualify as yet another example of metempsychosis, a word Molly Bloom stumbles over in the early part of the book. Barney Kiernan's pub, splendidly caught in Seán Lennon's line drawing, and which was given heroic proportions by Joyce as the 1904 equivalent of the Homeric Cyclops cave, lost half its bulk and dwindled into a unisex hairdressers shop in recent days. The building has now, I think, been entirely replaced. Moreover, not only is the Metropole Hotel, which I do not remember, gone, long vanished after the bombardment of O'Connell Street in 1916 and the devastation of the civil war but its replacement (the rather grand, opulent Metropole cinema, grill bar and ballroom, of which I have vivid memories) has also gone, replaced by some functional British based stores. There are changes even out on Gertie McDowell's Sandymount Strand although of a summer's evening one can still catch an echo of what the Edwardian scene here must have been like.

In any case Joyce does not give us very much in the way of architectural description. Instead *Ulysses*, as Seán Lennon himself has pointed out, is a highly accurate street map. Joyce's boast that the city of Dublin if destroyed could be rebuilt from the pages of his novel is incorrect. It could, however, be used to develop a very concise Ordnance Survey style of cartography.

Seán Lennon has caught in his delightful vignettes, aspects not just of Joyce's novel, but also of the irreverent view taken by Dubliners of great artists. This book has of course particular appeal for me because it revisits some of the haunts of my childhood such as Sandymount near my early home. How I remember Sandymount Green and the shop corner caught in one of the drawings with a curious accuracy. I remember the wall of Leverett and Fry's shop, that shop that possessed among other delights a gizmo for sending the change from the different counters to a central cash office by pulling a trigger and sending a little round container skating across the ceiling on wires. Or Batts the chemist shop on the other corner with its Dodge City/Wells Fargo style swing-doors. How often I went in there as a child to get a prescription filled with my fingers itching to draw an imaginary six shooter and paste the chemist's assistant into the wainscotting with a well aimed silver bullet. And then there is the Crampton Memorial around which the 52 bus used to make its laborious way when we went into town on shopping expeditions. This was a curious thing, like a genetically modified pineapple commemorating the exploits of a celebrated Irish Florist/Botanist called Crampton.

This is a book for enjoyment and fun. It concentrates principally on the funeral episode in which Paddy Dignam is laid to rest in Glasnevin Cemetery, having been transported from his home in Sandymount. In the James Joyce Centre we used to organise every Bloomsday a re-enactment of this episode. I attended many of them but on one occasion I was appearing in the theatre in Seville, doing my one-man show about Joyce's life and work, and telephoned home to find out how things were going. I got a breathless account of that year's re-enactment of the funeral. A horse-drawn, glass-sided hearse had been acquired, as well as the services of a professional jarvey who sat up on his box accompanied by one of James Joyce's grand-nephews, my friend Bob Joyce. His brother Derek took the role of the corpse and lay down comfortably in the coffin for the journey to the graveyard. However, when they got up near 'The Brian Boru' pub, the cortège stopped at a traffic light and Derek, feeling a bit stuffy in the box, lifted the lid of the coffin and sat up to look around and see where he was. A collection of old dears, out in a hired charabanc bus for an outing, fainted with shock and had to receive medical attention while the hearse took off lickety split to the graveyard where it took a sharp turn at considerable speed, the whole thing turned over, and the coffin shot out onto the verge spilling its contents onto the gravel. However, in a typically Joycean turn, the corpse survived unscathed but poor Bob Joyce, who came off the box in a heap, suffered a badly sprained ankle. I think uncle James would have smiled grimly to himself. These days horse-drawn funerals are becoming once again fashionable in the north inner city.

This little book proves that not only is there lots of fun to be had at Finnegans Wake, but also quite a good deal of innocent entertainment to be had by viewing Joyce's great novel through the eye of a gifted artist like Seán Lennon.

Author's Introduction

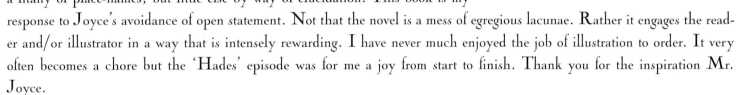

Despite the inclusion of 168 streets and over 200 buildings in *Ulysses* there is no great attempt on Joyce's part to physically describe Dublin. Some find his portrayal of the city ineffective. For Arnold Bennett, Joyce lacked 'geographical sense'. But Joyce's Dublin feels remarkably, intensely real even though he preferred suggestion and allusion to physical description. Which probably explains his appeal to visual artists. Perfectly rendered both topographically and psychologically, his city nevertheless remains featureless. Many of its streets are referred to by name only. Paddy Dignam's funeral route elicits a litany of place-names, but little else by way of elucidation. This book is my response to Joyce's avoidance of open statement. Not that the novel is a mess of egregious lacunae. Rather it engages the reader and/or illustrator in a way that is intensely rewarding. I have never much enjoyed the job of illustration to order. It very often becomes a chore but the 'Hades' episode was for me a joy from start to finish. Thank you for the inspiration Mr. Joyce.

As this is an adaptation, and a loose one at that, I have taken certain liberties throughout. The characters itineraries and the movement and places along the way of the funeral are more or less accurate to the novel. I have refrained from quoting the text however. Furthermore I have introduced 1 or 2 generic characters of my own. The gravediggers for example are borrowed from my last book, *Dublin Writers and Their Haunts*. I have also chosen to exaggerate, for dramatic effect, the length of the cortege. The activity in the cemetery is pretty much of my imagination, apart from the primary physical event of the burial.

Dubliners still harbour a residual begrudgery towards *Ulysses*. No doubt this has something to do with its banning, and subsequent unavailability. Today, when deviant behaviour is employed to sell everything from toilet rolls to toffee bars, its hard to know *what else* the fuss could have been about. Bad language perhaps? In Dublin? Perish the &%@!*$ thought! Could there possibly be a correlation between Joyce's work and the actual use by Dubliners of bad language (as distinct from the bad use of language)? In a country where literary skill is highly prized and your average citizen tends to have a free-for-all approach to verbal communication, its hardly surprising that Joyce's use of language could become an issue. By way of illustration and in conclusion of my introduction let me take you on two short, sharp odysseys of the lesser but true kind.

Aubrey crawls the grid locked streets of Dublin on behalf of Bus Eireann. Some time ago he told me the following story, on a 31, somewhere between the Bayside and Marino bus stops. While still at school one of his daughters, Patricia, took a summer job, her first ever, in Bewley's of Westmoreland Street. Cleaning tables one day she was approached by an elderly American couple on walkabout who appeared to be viewing the city through the cabbage-tinted lens of 'The Quiet Man'.

'Hi',they asked.

'Howyiz' says she.

'Vernon here', says the lady American, 'has a *critical condition*. He keeps gettin' this overpowerin' urge to eat. Could you recommend some place serving casual, rather than formal lunch?'

Not wishing to appear uninformed Patricia named the first pub to come into her mind.

'You could try "The Hoors Melt" (names have been changed to protect the innocent, just in case there's any left) in North Earl Street?'

In no time at all they'd scurried out the door. Like founding customers of an exciting new slaughterhouse they ran out before Patricia could warn them. About 'The Hoors Melt'. That it was one of the last great poisoning shops on the north side. And that the place was dangerous as well as infamous. And feared as much for the language of its clientele as for their random acts of violence.

Two anxiety-ridden weeks later Patricia informed her dad of the return of Madge and Vernon. There was no visible sign of butchering. Instead of two freezer-ready sides-of-tourist, if not half-porkers, a happy pair of visitors came to show their gratitude.

'Hey', they said in full-blooded two-part harmony.

'We simply gotta thank you for sendin' us there.'

'Oh you liked it?'

'We loved it! Y'see me an' Vernon belong to the Boston James Joyce Society. We ate at "The Hoors Melt" every day for a week an' you know what? In no time at all we were saying "please... pass the &@£!%! salt".'

⸺

Many years ago my beloved wife Anne and I travelled to the south side in order to raise the tone. We were making good time, not having been held up in customs, and decided to take a walk beside the sea in Killiney. Three female undergraduate types came towards us. The one in the middle pointed seaward saying:

'But of course it was Joyce who spoke of the sea-green snot'.

Always glad to be of assistance my intervention was swift and apposite and in the manner of Johnny Cash's 'Forty Shades Of Green Sea-Snot'.

(Due to circumstances beyond our control it is not possible to directly quote Jem the Penman. *Is Dona Linn An Briseadh Seo* so no need to get snotty.)

⸺

EPPS'S COCOA

Nelson Pillar

Site of
Plasto's

Daniel O'Connell

Dorset Street

Sackville St.
(now O'Con

Dunphy's Corner
(now Doyle's)

Brian Boru Pub

N.C.Rd

Eccles Street

Blessington
Street

Berkeley
Street

Glasnevin
Cemetery

Crossguns
Bridge

Dignam's
9 Newbridge Avenue

Irishtown
Road

Dodder Bridge

Ringsend Road

Grand Canal Bridge

National School

St. Andrew's

Great Brunswick Street (now Pearse)

Westland Row

THE QUEENS TH

Site of
Queens

D'Olier
Street

TCD

Campanile

Site of Crampton's Memorial

O'Connell Bridge

Dignam Funeral Route

Dramatis Personae in Ulysses

LEOPOLD BLOOM: 38 and Jewish although baptised into the Catholic church. Milly Bloom, his daughter, is 15. Rudy, his late son, died as an infant. Molly Bloom, his wife, is otherwise engaged. A diligent advertising canvasser, he is the original mollycoddler.

MOLLY BLOOM: Exotic, erotic and born in Gibraltar, she is the rock on which Leopold may yet perish. Molly is 33 and prefers meaningful monologue to dialogue.

STEPHEN DEDALUS: Something of an alter-ego for Joyce, to whom Dedalus is psychologically close. 22 and living at the Sandycove Martello tower, though not for long, he teaches history a mile away in Dalkey, where Joyce also taught.

The Sandycove Martello tower was built, like its fellow erection on Sandymount's Strand Road, in anticipation of Gallic aggression. However, the only significant incursion in its history was one involving members (and only three at that) of the huge cast of *Ulysses*.

Constructed on the Dublin coast between 1804-1806 along with twenty other Martellos, Sandycove may not have seen Old Boney or the Blownapart 'action' it was created for, but in 1904 the Napoleonic ego was just about made flesh when Buck Mulligan, modelled on Oliver St John Gogarty, initiated the novel's opening episode

Enter Stephen Dedalus and Haines (or their real-life counterparts Joyce and Samuel Chenevix Trench). They walk to the 'Forty Foot', a gentlemen's bathing place which may have been named after the Fortieth Foot Regiment.

Private School Dalkey

The private boys school where Stephen taught (like Joyce) was situated in a house on Dalkey Avenue at the corner with Old Quarry, known as 'Summerfield'.

In a fearless revelation of Stephen the outsider's inner life and thought process, as he walks by the sea, we are given to understand he has something a lot more substantial on his mind than taking a paddle.

Our first sighting of **L**eopold **B**loom, the wandering **O**dysseus reincarnate, is deceptively low-key, as he potters about the basement-kitchen of 7 **E**ccles **S**treet preparing **M**olly's breakfast and feeding the cat before feeding the wife.

Eccles Street

Named in 1772 after the Ulster family of Sir John Eccles, prior to the demolition of its north side Eccles Street was one of Georgian Dublin's finest. The front door of the immortal no.7 is currently preserved in the James Joyce Centre in North Great George's Street.

Dlugacz's

Let the gastro-literary odyssey begin! Leopold purchases a pork-kidney in Dlugaczs. Situated somewhere between St. Joseph's national school and Blessington Street, this pork butchers should prove hard to find as it is the only fictional Dublin shop in the novel.

There would be no need of a private detective in Molly Bloom's bedroom. Leopold, who notes his wife's resemblance to the nymph portrayed above her bed, eschews the truth of his private predicament and meets the louder signs of Molly's adultery with a non-organic loss of hearing.

Sandymount

What goes for the living Dubliner goes too, in terms of respect, for the dead. The late morning of 16 June 1904 involves the funeral of a Paddy Dignam, proceeding to Glasnevin cemetery from picturesque Sandymount (so pretty that even the gravediggers and undertakers take the 'scenic route' before assembling at Dignam's to practice their dying art).

Signalling time's final triumph, the moment has come for the mourners (just as it has gone, alas, for Paddy). At about 11am the funeral starts off from the Dignam family home at 9 Newbridge Avenue in the then maritime Sandymount.

Attending his friends funeral, and pondering its implications, is Bloom who shares a tight-fit carriage with Martin Cunningham, Jack Power and Simon Dedalus. In the previous century the avenue was known as 'Haig's Lane' after a tax-dodging distiller. Patrick Pearse's family lived at number 3 up to 1900.

The hearse and carriages turn left on Tritonville Road. Tritonville Lodge, at the junction of Tritonville Road with Newbridge Avenue and Sandymount Road, was first built in 1796.

At once Sandymount's southern and Ringsend's northern portion, Irishtown is said to have had the first hot water pool in Ireland. Advertised as 'close to Tritonville Road', Cranfield's Baths, to which a tram travelled 'every 10 minutes', promised a 'constant and unlimited supply of pure sea water' to be 'pumped in direct by steam power'.

Comparisons may be as odious as Poolbeg-generated air is malodorous (to this olfactory at least) but Irishtown has held its own with both neighbours, Sandymount and Ringsend. As the mourners travel along Irishtown Road many pedestrians raise their hats as a show of respect.

Bloom spots Stephen among the passers by, and his father Simon Dedalus delivers a rant against the roguish Buck Mulligan.
Soon they are proceeding into Ringsend.

This beautiful towering landmark of a church overlooking the hump-backed bridge is not quite an integral part of the story as it was not erected until 1912! It is however an integral part of my rendering of the hump-backed bridge, and very *dathúil*, if I say so myself.

Ringsend

In 1837 Samuel Lewis wrote of Ringsend's 'mean and dilapidated appearance'. Weston St. John Joyce said it was 'decayed and unattractive'. Even in Joyce's time, Ringsend or 'the point of the tide' at which the Dodder meets the Liffey, had seen better days. These may have gone with the packet boats, long after the last one was moored there, but Ringsend endures today amid signs of a real renaissance.

The granite bridge over the Dodder (officially titled **Charlotte Bridge**) was built in 1803, following floods. This was the first permanent bridge and replaced previous unsuccessful timber efforts on the same site.

The funeral carriages stop at the Grand Canal Bridge, with Boland's Mill to its left. The influence of Homer on *Ulysses* is clearly seen here. In *The Odyssey* Odysseus did not relish the prospect of his visit to the 'kingdom of the dead'. Leopold is also trepidatious and on his journey to Glasnevin crosses the Dodder, Grand Canal, Liffey and Royal Canal waterways, which correspond to the four rivers of the underworld.

The cortege then proceeds through Great Brunswick Street, which in 1923 was renamed Pearse Street.

Built no later than the middle of the 19th century, this is the longest terrace on Great Brunswick Street. The Doric columns framing the doorcase of 184 are echoed by smaller columns dividing the door, and wonderful to see.

Queen's Theatre

An historic Dublin theatre, the Queen's was originally built in 1844 at no.209 Great Brunswick Street, on the site of a previous theatre, the Adelphi, and leased by Trinity College. It was redesigned several times, and developed to include nos.207-211. The Queen's became the home of the Abbey company from 1951–1966 following a fire at their theatre.

Joyce's reference to Plasto's of Great Brunswick Street consists of a one-word phrase which happens to be the fourth word in this sentence.

Constructed in 1832 this was, among other things, a famous seafood restaurant preferred by the Irish literati. More recently the Congregation of the Blessed Sacrament opened a chapel on the building's ground floor. Leopold's response to the sighting of Blazes Boylan is described by Harry Blamires as 'a miracle of Joycean economy and pathos'.

Crampton's Memorial

This bizarre gazebo was intended as a tribute to Sir Philip Crampton, a Victorian surgeon and founder-member of the Royal Zoological Society. Standing on the corner of College Street and Hawkins Street, its bust of Crampton surrounded by three swans with water-font lions in full spate under a botanical stairway to pineapple heaven would have made you want to pull up a bollard and sit down.

At O'Connell Bridge the cab approaches the third waterway as the horrors of the underworld (and not just the north side!) draw ever closer.

Anna Livia

Leopold would not have been sanguine passing over Anna Livia, a corruption by the Normans of the native *Abhann na Life*, or river Liffey. O'Connell Street corruptions are not that uncommon today. The stiletto in the ghetto and the tart with the cart still do nicely.

Time is the ultimate explicator and so the Liberator meets the Terminator as the funeral procession of Paddy Dignam, recently deceased, goes by the Daniel O'Connell Monument, erected in 1874, and still standing.

Originally called Drogheda Street but renamed Sackville Street after substantial widening and remodelling, by Luke Gardiner in the 1750s, transformed it into a finer quality residential street. The first mention of O`Connell Street was in 1884 but not officially until 1924, although it began to commercialise as a street in the 19th century. Today, the street seems to belong to Dublin`s consumer-driven chisellers, wantonly in search of their consumer-group peers.

The Hely's men take a break. The old Hotel Metropole was embedded in the heart of Dublin's premier street but got caught in the general devastation of 1916. It was replaced by the Metropole cinema and restaurant. Marvellously inviting and always smelling of good food I loved to go there as a boy.

The Nelson Pillar was a well established part of Sackville Street when a porch was added at street level in 1894. Sackville Street was vigorously commercial when Carlisle Bridge was dramatically widened in 1880. Hawkers were a common sight and sound around the pillar and Joyce records the plaintive voice of a native plum-seller at full cry as the mourners pass.

The dead dominate the living in this episode and death becomes a major preoccupation at this stage of the journey. Even the less interesting aspect of Upper Sackville's west side affects Bloom, as he considers it bereft of life. The Gresham Hotel at nos. 21–22 on the east side, is where Gabriel and Gretta Conroy stay in 'The Dead'.

Rotunda Concert Rooms

These were built 1764-1786 to facilitate banquets and other fund raising entertainments on behalf of the new Lying-in hospital.

The procession keeps straight on up North Frederick Street from Great Britain Street, renamed Parnell Street in 1911. In 1802 *Wilson's Dublin Directory* was published by a William Corbett of no.57 Great Britain Street. Following a takeover it became *Thom's Dublin Directory*. In his obituary for Joyce, C.P. Curran wrote 'Joyce was many things, but he was certainly the last 40 volumes of *Thom's Directory* thinking aloud'.

The carriage, having passed Findlater's Church keeps straight on from North Frederick Street, crossing Dorset Street to Blessington Street where it gathers pace.

Prior to drawing them, I checked out the Blessington and Berkeley streets on a Wednesday in early March. Walking back along the car-filled Ballybough road with all thoughts centred on the funeral of Dignam, I heard first the sound of wheels turning followed by a trotting of hoofs and was passed by a horse-drawn hearse, in what felt like a direct affirmation from the great animator Himself.

Turning a corner the funeral procession, or at least its front part, is brought to a halt by cattle-herding along the North Circular Road. This practice continued on the capital's streets well into the 1960s.

Still a landmark, this corner is now known as Doyle's Corner. The cabs turn right at Dunphy's onto Phibsborough Road.

Crossguns Bridge

At Crossguns bridge the carriages reach the fourth and final waterway thus completing Leopold's approach by water to the terrors of Hades.

They pass 'The Brian Boru', a public house dedicated to the memory of an ancient but dead High King of Ireland.
He died at the hands of a Dane in 1014, and not as a result of drinking a bad pint.

The mourners approach the graveyard through a development of houses before passing the scene of the then infamous Thomas Childs murder of 1899.

They arrive at Glasnevin Cemetery originally known as Prospect. If a Dubliner describes Glasnevin as 'a bit dead' you can be sure this is not intended as a serious comment on the provision of social amenities in the area. At one hundred and twenty acres it is the largest cemetery in Ireland. The watchtowers and the O'Connell memorial round tower are among its most remarkable features.

Bodysnatchers

From 1792, when medical science began to reward sticklers for their attention paid to anatomical detail, the dark practice of disinterring and stealing bodies suitable for dissection became a lucrative vocation. The professionals in the field were called 'resurrectionists' or 'sack-em-ups'. As a result watchtowers were built, and Cuban bloodhounds released nocturnally, for the benefit of Glasnevin's newly interred.

The approach to the cemetery is dominated by the round tower. It was designed by George Petrie, the antiquarian and artist, who had a special interest in ecclesiastical architecture. The mourners walk inside after the coffin.

Chapel

J. J. McCarthy, the outstanding 'Irish Gothic' architect, designed the chapel. The coffin is shouldered into the mortuary chapel. After the service, the coffin is taken out of the chapel on a coffin-cart.

Dignam's Grave

Joyce does not specify the precise location of Dignam's grave. The following is my alternative 'extra-textual' route…

Who knows what inspires people in their choice of memorial? In the case of successful merchant class and business folk might not a close association with their best-selling product find an echo in the symbols and styles employed in their monuments?

The table tomb was an eminently practical attempt to avoid the visible affects of nature's cycle of death and rebirth (with hopefully the odd game of chance squeezed in between the two).

Funeral Origins

Dignam's funeral, though fictitious, was based on the actual funeral of Matthew F. Kane, an unfortunate Dubliner who died in tragic circumstances on 10 July 1904 and is also buried in Glasnevin. Bloom's experience of 'Hades' is intensified by his predicament as a Jewish man attending a Roman Catholic funeral.

Mount Jerome came to Glasnevin for this one. Monuments on the grand scale are now a thing of the past. Irish monumental artists, like their counterparts in architecture, were a modest bunch who rarely tried to match the majesty of *Cimetiére du Pêre Lachaise*'s funerary edifices. Furthermore, in Ireland the wake was always given priority.

Bloom's interior monologue is totally at odds with the dialogue of his fellow mourners. His grounding into the underworld is via his personal isolation. By the graveside he notices the mysterious 'Macintosh', the question of whose identity has for years driven Joyceans around the twist. It has even been suggested that the mystery mourner is Joyce himself.

Hynes and Mr. Power visit the grave of Parnell before leaving the cemetery. The 'Chief' is still commemorated on 'Ivy Day' of every year.

The mourners pass through the gates, happy to forget a potent reminder of their own mortality. Perhaps they pick up speed, all the quicker to leave behind thoughts of coffins, corpses and gravediggers. Time moves on inexorably if only to overtake the undertakers.

Having already traced the early morning rituals of Stephen Dedalus and Bloom, we get to learn about their routine day after Dignam's funeral. At two o'clock Stephen enters the National Library.

The oratorical encounter between Stephen Dedalus and a scholarly group of fat-chewers takes place in the office of William Lyster, the librarian. But what if it had begun in the Reading Room?

Barney Kiernan's pub in Little Britain Street is the setting for the best known pub scene in *Ulysses*. It was known as the 'Court of Appeal' due to its proximity to the Four Courts. Since the funeral Bloom has placed an ad at the Freeman's Journal, lunched at Davy Byrnes, avoided Boylan, met Stephen at the National Library, and followed Boylan to the Ormond Hotel. It is five o`clock and for Bloom the long day wanes.

Bloom, following Stephen, enters Nighttown via Mabbot (or Corporation) Street.

Concerned for the inebriated and vulnerable Stephen, Bloom brings him back to no.7 where they make contact over a grand cup of Epps's soluble cocoa, before Stephen departs.

Molly gives her famous sixty-page monologue containing enough examples of the 'yes' word to carry any national referendum.

When asked what he was thinking of while posing in 1904 for what has become his best-known photograph, Joyce replied that he was weighing up his chances of borrowing five shillings from the photographer, Constantine P. Curran. It is interesting to speculate how Joyce might have disposed of the money on *that* day in June 1904...

Perhaps he started mid-morning, by taking the sea-air in Kingstown, for his constitutional…

And then caught the Dalkey tram all the way back to the centre of Dublin…

Where, on North Earl Street off Sackville Street at the Pillar, he buys a bunch of flowers…

Having crossed O'Connell Bridge he makes straight for Foster Place to, no doubt, do something he could only do in a Bank, like lodge a shilling…

Passing the statue of Grattan, he crosses Dame Street where Tom Kernan works at no.5 for Pulbrook,
Robertson and Co…

Moving along he notices the railings of Trinity College, and its fine neo-classical façade for which he had little regard…

He stands on the corner of Grafton Street and Nassau Street, across from where Bloom checked prices at Yeates and Son…

83

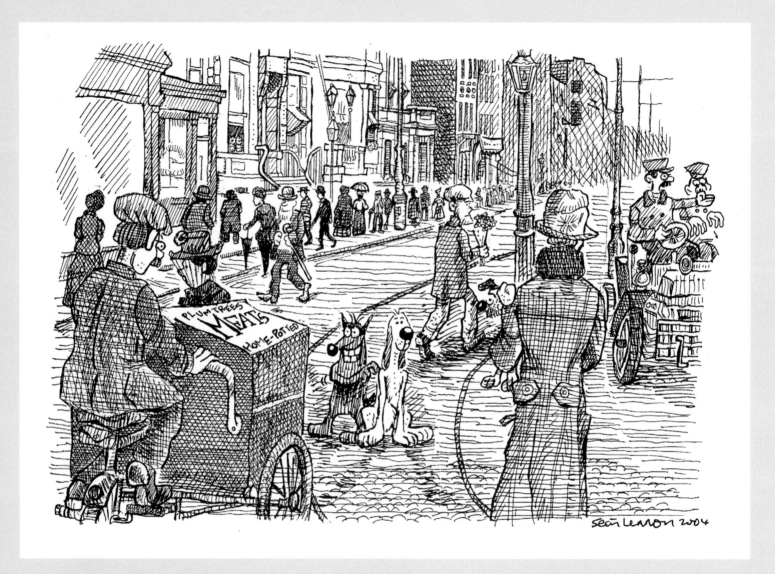

Unlike Lenehan who walked in turmoil about the Green, a man alone, James walks with a certain *je ne sais quoi*, a certain *níl fhios agam*.

On the corner of Merrion Square he sees the woman for whom he will immortalise this day forever…

......as you might do for one you love.

I hope without sense
to breathe dead fragrance.

The odour died when it was born.
This rusty graveyard gate
says what I cannot: *forlorn*.
A weird moan. I am too late.

From *Flüntern* by Alan Moore

Bibliography

Armstrong, Alice, *The Joyce Of Cooking*. New York : Station Hill Press 1986

Bardon, C. & J., *If Ever You Go To Dublin Town*. Belfast : Blackstaff 1988

Bennett, Douglas, *Encyclopaedia Of Dublin*. Dublin : Gill & MacMillan 1991

Bidwell & Heffer, *The Joycean Way*. Dublin : Wolfhound Press 1981

Blamires, Harry, *The New Bloomsday Book*. London : Routledge 1966

Butler, David, *An Aid To Reading Ulysses*. Dublin : James Joyce Centre 2004

Cato & Vitiello, *Joyce Images*. London : Norton & Co. 1994

Death And Design In Victorian Glasnevin. Dublin Cemeteries Committee 2000

Freund & Carleton, *James Joyce In Paris*. London : Cassell 1965

Glasnevin Cemetery. Dublin Cemeteries Committee 1997

Gorham, Maurice, *Dublin From Old Photographs*. London : B.T. Batsford 1972

Gorham, Maurice, *Dublin Old & New*. Wakefield : EP Publishing 1975

Hart & Knuth, *A Topographical Guide To James Joyce's Ulysses*. Colchester : Wake Newslitter 1975

Hickey, Kieran, *Faithful Departed*. Dublin : Ward River Press 1982

Johnston, Lucy, *Dublin ~ Then And Now*. Dublin : Gill & MacMillan 1991

McCabe & Le Garsmeur, *James Joyce ~ Reflections Of Ireland*. London : Little, Brown & Co. 1993

Moore, Alan, *Opia*. London : Anvil Press 1986

Nicholson, Robert, *The Ulysses Guide*. London : Methuen 1988

O'Broin & McMahon, *Faces Of Old Leinster*. Belfast : Appletree Press 1978

Pearl, Cyril, *Dublin In Bloomtime*. London : Angus & Robertson 1969

Pierce, David, *James Joyce's Ireland*. New Haven : Yale U. P. 1992

Quinn, Edward, *James Joyce's Dublin*. London : Secker & Warburg 1974